X-RAYS
AND OTHER
LANDSCAPES

Also by Kyle McCord

Magpies in the Valley of Oleanders (2016)—Trio House
You Are Indeed an Elk, But This Is Not the Forest You Were Born to Graze
    (2015)—Gold Wake Press
Sympathy from the Devil (2013)—Gold Wake Press
Informal Invitations to a Traveler (2011)—Gold Wake Press
Galley of the Beloved in Torment (2011)—Dream Horse Press

X-Rays and
Other Landscapes

Poems by Kyle McCord

To Emmy,
Hope you dig
the book! Keep
putting dance on
the page!

THP

McCord, Kyle
1st edition.

ISBN: 978-1-9494870-2-2
Library of Congress Control Number: 2018951421

Interior Layout by Lea C. Deschenes
Cover Design by Nick Courtright
Editing by Matt Mauch and Tayve Neese

Printed in Tennessee, USA
Trio House Press, Inc.
Ponte Vedra Beach, FL

To contact the author, send an email to tayveneese@gmail.com.

GOLD WAKE

Reading

Friday, March 29th from 3:00-6:00
@ Ristretto Roasters
555 NE. Couch St.
short walk from the Convention Center)

Brandon Amico
Kyle Flak
Frances Cannon
Dana Diehl and Melissa Goodrich
Kelly Magee
David Wojciechowski
Nick Courtright

TABLE OF CONTENTS

I.

My Father Considering
His Brain Scan   3

Self-Portrait at Eighteen
Revisited at Thirty   5

Ephemera   7

Viewing *The Tribute Money*,
My Father Thinks of His Wife   9

On Size and Scope
in *The Arnolfini Portrait*   11

Tarrare after the Hospital   13

Chemo   15

My Father Considering
His Brain Scan as Lunar Disaster   17

Envisioning My Grandfather
in the Shadow
of Hopper's Lighthouse   19

Rain, Steam, and Speed   21

II.

Portrait of a Sideswiped Doe   25

I Consider My Father's
Brain Scan as Jazz Measure   26

Deaths of the Virgin   28

The Girl Picking Verbena
in the Valley Below
the Tower of Babel   30

On the Drive Home
from My Father's Surgery   32

A Lesson in Drawing   34

My Father Considering
His Brain Scan
as the Moon Titan   36

Self-Portrait as Butcher   38

Gas Leak Shutters
Furries Convention   40

Portrait of Lost Glasses   42

III.

Elegy After *The Sea of Ice*, 1823   47

Father's Brain Scan Seen
as Bomber Cutaway Model
and Bomber History   48

Watching Hoarders
with My Father   50

Self-Portrait
with Dog Crapping in Snow   52

Drawing Whistler's Mother   53

Watching a Cialis Ad
with My Father   55

Something Beautiful   56

Still-Life after New Year's
with Toy Boat   58

Portrait of My Grandfather
in Haiti   60

A Guide to Falling Down Stairs   62

Notes   65

Acknowledgements   67

I.

My Father Considering His Brain Scan

No clouds just the wickless horizon
like a Rothko black on black

an unfeeling wall of pigment
why not junipers here

why not wands of cowbane and waterdock
tracing riverbeds on the leaden hill

it's tough not to read this
dark matter as allegory

my cancer is thick and undulating
the invisible weight of nebulas

what part of me is left in this image
let's redraft

think Seurat's *Grande Jatte*—
a young mother to parade

swarming leaves
the yacht doubled

and swimming in the waters
children who will not be mastered—

anything but what is there reality
so dull when one can bargain with paint—

the boy whose swan body could carry him
far beyond the canvas ship

if only these winds were fair if only
these waters would still

the boy could outswim this current
I would paint him crabapples

fallen in a ditch eat of them
boy and know nothing

Self-Portrait at Eighteen Revisited at Thirty

Let me rinse your blue hair cut
your bleached tips and butter
your scalp with balm from the pharmacy
they'll call the cops if you show
so I'll foot the bill I'll drive
the Lincoln since it's past 10:30
I'll clean the pillow you ruined
writing violets purple martins with cheap dye
and restlessness the landscape
of your sleep mapped in stains
hang onto one of these
honor it like a flag and
burn it when you turn twenty-one
these love letters won't mean much now
sorry in advance for the bloody seam
on your left thigh see how it winds
like a garden snake halved with a hoe
sorry for how badly it hurts
to watch the next one in your rearview
I don't want to give anything away
but here's a pencil and some paper
here's a box of Kleenex and a laptop
full of porn I recommend the chicken
ginger let me walk you to your car
you're drunk where are your keys
later when you write all this down
those are narcissus those are egrets
the word you're looking for
is *pobrecita* the phrase you mean
to write is *I know now I will love*
which isn't false but let's get you

presentable boy because we only
have twelve years to break you open
leave you in a ditch somewhere
and see what crawls out

EPHEMERA

My father wanted golden lions
    the size of Pomeranians

to guard the house and he found them
    on a daytrip to the Ozarks—

a roadside stand down the path
    from a collapsed plantation

where manure carried through the wind-
    break's teeth through a picturesque

graveyard littered with dolls:
    row upon row of bronzed bobcats

chipmunks elephants whose trunks
    thick as a child's lisp beckoned

the lot reeked of cow dung
    but what a marvel:

a mile of lions
    lounged in uneasy array—

imagine the hours shaping pewter chipping
    out eyes sanding tails round

as worn biceps wouldn't you think
    someone would have stopped him

a son like me a wife like mom but no they lined
    the acre with monuments to obsession

and soon Sunday afternoons meant
　　for baling roasted in the kiln's fire—

the son watching *Salem's Lot*
　　on the old couch curled into himself

remained that way until morning—
　　he helped us hitch the two lions

to the Aerostar's roof and as the sun
　　measured shadows on the lot we surveyed

legions of antelope clustered
　　in a rain ditch the Lord's hand

obsessively and viciously
　　blessing the grass

Viewing *The Tribute Money,* My Father Thinks of His Wife

First notice how the loadstone nimbi
    weigh down it's what Massacio wanted—

the clouds the denuded
    foothills pressed beneath the sky
      it's the bleak hour

of sundown when dinner is over
    the twenty-tongued waters pull
      at the cedars

where are all the women
    why not a flush of kaolinite
      a mother washing her boy's fat belly

in resinous light but instead
    we are stuck under this unbearable
    oneness of sky and sea sea
      and the fish which sparkles

and knows it will die
    choking oxygen which tastes of flame
      which tastes porous but sweet

where are the nursing
    mothers the old mothers
we waste ourselves
    on anything less than women
      the opinions of old stubborn men
      even the miracle of frothy copper

fished from lips are like nothing
      next to her
      every night I'd watch her

walk out of the Adriatic I would
      stay on the deck
          where shearwaters levied tribute
          from the gargantuan trees

she would hum coring pears
      giving song unto song rending
          seed from stem rendering nothing
          to man or God

On Size and Scope
in *The Arnolfini Portrait*

The pregnant woman's arms are heavy
       as stone cookware and ache powerfully

better to be the dog
       slavering over marrow

she thinks better a cobble a figment
       not the round observatory

of the unborn what but a woman
       must carry another world
          inside her body

without complaint though if it isn't nausea
       it's insomnia

at night she can see
       stars pushing through the swelling dark
          crowning crowning
              over the cathedral

damn their luck damn the painter's
       gaunt fingers the monstrous deer
          treading the hill like monks

who've stumbled onto holy ground
       such grace in their strides

once she cried
       for one doe's rumpled
          hide over its womb

the creature's panic so
      familiar
           she watched her testing the weight
             of half-rotten fruit
            the deer glanced up

as if seeking blessing she struggled
      to remember a psalm
         as the deer panteth for the apple ...

her husband scribbled away
      while the doe's eyes never left her
        as flesh and fruit
           dripped from its mouth

both of us filled she thought
      heavy with hunger's gravity

TARRARE AFTER THE HOSPITAL

Tarrare (1772-1798) was a French showman, soldier, and curiosity who ate rocks, live cats, and snakes. Despite his relatively normal size, he was insatiably hungry at all time. He was admitted to a hospital where he scavenged for offal and tried to drink other patients' blood and eat from corpses in the morgue. After undergoing numerous failed diets to reduce his appetite, he was ejected from the hospital after suspicion grew that he had eaten a toddler.

Monstrosity begins in the guts
      tonight nothing satiates I snap
           the necks of two stray dogs
just to wind entrails round my fist
      one mutt fights I suck

my blood from its canines
      for my next trick I drink
           myself from storm drains
      let no drop of me escape
this country where I am
           a serpent on the tongue
           a banquet of moonstones
a firing squad a noose
bring them I am

ready just no more or much
      more wine vinegar
a black lung's share of tobacco
      could not dull drags me
through rank alley after
      dump into the grinding Seine

      between the water's teeth
its stink as fetid
      as the garbage I eat
a boy watches

the water snatches his reflection
      as it holds him under
ice refuses
      to expel what it swallows
what it can't ever truly admit
         (I swear it I never touched him)
     no it crowns the child back
into water's gorge

CHEMO

The man dreams of a waterpark
a boy with a tube splashes

in an artificial river what a day
he's having what a lark

raising the water in baptism
over the daddy late summer

light searches clavicle pelvis
the father's worried hands

in the clam-shaped tide pool
everyone is having fun

and no one cries over his father's
x-rays at the nurse's station

the sun-sweet clouds tussle over
the boy and his father until

the waves shunt them apart
send the father ahead so the boy

bobs distantly behind him
in the water's course like the tail

of a puppy now the boy wails
joyous with the thrill

of gravity's pulse and
the father you can see it

by his darting eyes
is worried to go over the drop ahead

is worried to let the child second him
but the boy is just a wavelet yet

and so many others already
wait in the tide pool

so what's to worry
incendiary blaze tinges

his hairy chest his bald head
the machine roar

of the churning swill
he plunges *goodbye*

daddy shouts the boy
goodbye!

My Father Considering His Brain Scan as Lunar Disaster

The night after I was diagnosed
        I dreamed I was jettisoned into space
                where mysteriously alive I passed

prolonged time
        so many years
        swimming unable to breathe or
                to record the downpour

of diamonds on Neptune
        Io's restless tides

mostly the limitless
        pitch beyond Ceres I remember

your mother's
        voice calling me back to earth back

to die indentured to my own
        gravity my native darkness
                my street our house

how to come home I asked myself

too far in this one direction
        powerless to stop this pull
                down toward whatever
                        (I can't say

I cared) *imagine*
our neighbors the voice said

their empty studies
    how they would draw open their windows
      smoke cloves think
        of the sweet odor

how it must have felt
    to touch those red dwarves to their lips

though I knew those lights
    that reached me
      were already gone

Envisioning My Grandfather in the Shadow of Hopper's Lighthouse

It's an old voice coming back
      the footpath parched to rot
           by winter's late puberty

the voice of the town pastor
      my grandfather
           his cologne is the cling

of pipe tobacco
      he is carrying a basket of reels
           he's found more cheap gold rings

to imprint on a child's wrist
      on a lippy woman's face—
           my mother more than once—

the fever dream of afternoon
      breaks into cinnamon
           across the gulch of Russian sage

in the museum where drafts
      are mutters below the breath
           (think of the onlookers at Woolworth's

when she paused too long
      at the makeup counter)
           I imagine him wheeling around

that impossible clime
      the reels teeter between
            digits of a hand which pats

the Testament tucked in a shirt pocket
      maybe he's come to be forgiven
            his solitude which kept him

distant as subject from audience
      whatever pain he carried
            back from the Pacific like a trophy

wait here while I work my way among the Rodins
      upstairs the statuary fills with families
            the blasphemy of their bodies

isn't the pain they hold
      but what they conceal—
            massacres and patricides

no stone skin can show
      I turn the corner and here he is too
            with a dark-haired boy frightened

and frantic for a bathroom
      my grandfather stares down at him
            as he journeys to the edge of perspective

with a familiar malice
      with the boy's hand trembling in his
            though I imagine he'd rather without

Rain, Steam, and Speed

For these boys it's the closest they'll come
    to church genuflected beyond

the tree line a vestibule where jewelweed
    and foxglove needle hairless
limbs goosebumps rise
    on their eager skin one giggles
    and is mothered

back to reverence
    they are a verge of gibbering flies
    then the rumble trembles dew

soggy clover the flowers are weak
    petitioners brought to their knees

this train like Turner's
    Pentecostal tongue pieces them

oh hands oh sides weak as India paper
    it closes on the epileptic rail
    they are mad with its power

and it's then the youngest sees
    his grubby penny tip off the rail

to be nothing itself
    and suddenly he is up
    and racing

what happens next
    is a story in figures and fingers
    too easy to sever maybe

he will close the distance
        oh boy rising toward
                this pauper's alter make it

the other boys scream
        to move back there will be
                more days like this they are shrill

because who can say the wheels will settle
        at the knuckle at the wrist

we want it to be less
        the train so close now
                I want to unwrite what brought him here

but what whets like blood
        and this verse does not ask a wrist
but a whole boy
                the only whom we love

II.

Portrait of a Sideswiped Doe

She's unhurt and
     stunned limps behind an ash

what's happened
     to the glade

each trunk an unshattered
     femur the very hide

of ragged wood: skinned
     so all's anew

she stoops to gnaw trembling
     a cut between blunted teeth

her shaking pitiable
     adrenaline souring

even the taste of cud
     so the meadow's rattle

and chug honeysuckle
     thick as motor oil are

what's averted
     so a voice magically

raises the geese
     hollow as clouds

they watch her
     wander deeper into the wood

wait for it to work some
     docile shape

I Consider My Father's Brain Scan as Jazz Measure

How could you work with what was given you
to paint with spasms thick as the ride

on "Groovin' Hard" ever approaching total stillness
as it slowed through your studio's speakers

an asymptote approximation of form now gone
Buddy Rich played on as the shadow of a needle

and as we sat listening in those lawn chairs
you grew lean your dendroid arms

your unfamiliar face suddenly blank
your eyes traced specters on canvas the ghost

notes you hummed you knew by heart Armstrong
even Rakha you'd read the charts *But to have everything*

written out for you it's not really creating
said Buddy in an interview

you wrote that on scrap paper
pinned it to the wall beside the picture of me

on the Vic Firth set you couldn't afford
you lifted yourself from your seat

set out bottles of acrylics made your rumpled
mat beside the CD changer

where after you'd gone I punched through drywall—
how you wouldn't listen how to work with that—

with spasms timely as an entrance
broken muscles who dying insist on song

Deaths of the Virgin

Caravaggio lover of whores
        painted one's face
                on the mother of God

or at least that's what the monks said
        who tossed it out of the chapel
                not just because she was a whore

but because she was real
        not in the way they imagined:

her skin sickly as wheat in winter
        her hands cracked like a common
                woman spading weeds in noon light

she should have been an empress in a flock
        of radiant garments should
                have been *their* Mary

who would bow to this
        harlot they wondered

but the artist incarnated her
        the way only a pupil of the body
                could—her face an apparition
                    of a lover

hands like snow birds suddenly
        rising into storm

and hadn't the monks conjured
       their own virgin from mothers
             or a maid's daughter freed from work
           bundling oats

whose Mary have I taken
       they might have asked
             before yanking the portrait
               from the chapel façade

to the women who watched
       this must have been a familiar violence

the painting squalled as they freed it
       like a woman dragged across cobbles
           by her hair

The Girl Picking Verbena in the Valley Below the Tower of Babel

She doesn't know beauty dies
faster when she snaps the sepal sharp
like a hen for butchering

she's seen mother do it
gore on her hands and after
they chanted over oolong leaves

for fertility she repeats the ritual
to herself but can't augur what
comes next—how the forest deep

as an abscess merely operates as
a metaphor for the shadow
of something grand and toppling

her body changing in this
vortex of nettles secretly
eager to grope and sting

the sum of branches planish
while she whispers language
to the unspeaking verbena

to this wild shaded by Bruegel
so it is presence and absence
it spills around her as some sign

of arcades soon to crumble
under absolute wrath
but she will always be on the brink

of this storm always imminently
a woman trapped as a girl
picking fabricated garlands

a shorthand for something else
as so much sketched in the margin
by an old man's brush

how merciful of the artist to save
her from errors of the body these thick
tongues going down as fire

On the Drive Home
from My Father's Surgery

A gown of lichen clothes the glen
      where catfish gum mosquitos

from the lacey shallows it's no challenge
      to imagine a bog wench surfacing

from the muck a rotten vixen
      like the one Jack fondles

in *The Shining* such a trip
      when he stumbles back from

the grinning skeleton can you fathom
      the stink if you're Jack

then you know it's all true too
      an afterlife but no new body

same cage of sinews same
      yoyo of intestines waiting to unwind

what's the point really
      all this bitterness you've sharpened

in the whiskey light of winter
      a total bust when only you're to blame

might as well play the minotaur let snow's
      teeth grind you to powder

now you're an obelisk a simulacrum
        of your own insanity

what does the ghost say then
        looking into its own frozen eye

how kind you were
        to carry me inside you

I should have buttoned that coat
        I should have loosed that ax

A Lesson in Drawing

Notice the turbine
    and the coven of pines

they're so sober the pencil lines
    divide subject from the rest of the landscape

what are we to make
    of the young man meandering
        toward the college metal shop
in his ill-fitting jacket
    you can see he's fingering the bulge
    of a handgun

he looks to hardly
    be moving at all
    sluggish lazy like a boy
        swaying in the sheets
        in the 4 AM dark

next consider how we came
    to this vantage

consider who we are
    we're migratory birds
        or a news chopper hovering

because there is a story here
    in x-rays and landscapes simplified

so the boy is the failure
    the Colt is a tool
        which is one type of truth

another: the gun show and the trailer
            the opened bottle of lithium
                        each pill stamped into the carpet

like the butts of Lucky Strikes
            on the cracking steps
                        of the gymnasium

            where the congressman is holding
                        up the AR-15 to the crowd

roaring into the microphone
            and the boy claps with this mass
            (not pictured here)

but art is also its shadow
            (write that down) warns
                        if we don't know we're not looking

deep enough now think
            what the boy sees

when he stares back
            back at us who are another gallery

whatever we are to him we are here
            to watch we are leaves
            like desiccated steamers
                        open gullet of

river nothing he can touch

My Father Considering
His Brain Scan
as the Moon Titan

It burns blue as the gas lamp's flame
a tedious fly orbits lured by the crackle

of backlight *what comes next* asks Sarah
but isn't this a map with an end in mind

(cartography of a place we can't touch
its rivers of methane rivers of cyanide)

the fly lands feeling the contours of the x-ray
for the origin of all this brightness

this means more tests of course more blood
samples and drips of poison

in the waiting room impressionistic
giraffes someone's son leafs

through *National Geographic*
scientists believe life began in the icy

shallows of Titan then fanned out
ferried below glacial expanses

meteorites might have carried these
micro-organisms across the cosmos

how can anyone be sure this far away
the clouds could be anything—

a blanket spread for a picnic
with a father and his daughter

who could pass the evening
guessing childish names

for the furious and arcane stars
small and hard as pills

Self-Portrait as Butcher

After *Judith Beheading Holofernes*

Grisly so vicious I can't forget
        how casually the women
                rolled up their sleeves this was business

not pleasure
        but some pleasure
                in it still Artemisia

has not forgotten that
        while shaving I reread their faces
                so virago cool *a man no different*

from a heifer becomes
        chuck and offal say the pupils
                their faces are butcher's

paper empathy rolling off
        like a tide of lather sliced
                bloodless down my chin

what man did you hate
        this much Artemisia to cut
                him forever like that

how rusted that bastard
        sword must be now but
                here is their cruelty

recorded in oily oscuro
        like the blood-flared cloud
                scudding the clogged drain

it won't dissolve and I know
      for certain I'm not capable of this
         the lemon-scented soap

washes nothing fully
      from my shaking hands
         the grotesque tool

leaves a dirty shallow
      I try to find my own face
         in that mirror

but there is an old maid's
      an alien hand steady and
         carving flesh

Gas Leak Shutters
Furries Convention

Consider my student who wanted
      to be someone else or something else
         wanted to be the whitetails

his father brought down each spring
      the two of them hunkered
         in a tree stand

invisible they shared a pack
      of Lucky Strikes swigged sour beer

how odd that he wrote an essay as an animal
      the musky body of a deer suit
         he rented for Furryfest Dallas

he attended panels scrawled
      illegible notes in mammoth letters—

like a museum in which all the art
      is touchable he wrote subheading:
         finding a fur friendly workplace
            subheading: *coming out to family*

he didn't pretend it was his first
      I could nearly feel the silky fan
         of shame he'd hidden

some hundred times until he hadn't
      I could imagine the surge of adrenaline

when his father a West Texas pipeline worker
        shoved him against the plywood
                pulled off his mother's pearls

lipstick smeared like a trickle
        of blood from a backhand
                no son of mine he said
                        and wound back

I wanted to be anybody
        but you dad

wrote the boy
        there's a taste anger leaves
                and sometimes all you can do is spit

today when I open the tribune to read
        this story what's shocking
                isn't my student holding the matted
                        brown orb of his head in the crook of his arm

what's shocking is how
        the caption calls this a mask—

the bear's worn countenance
        which doesn't look like any man

PORTRAIT OF LOST GLASSES

The glasses at pool's bottom
       want to flap their featherless
wings but the water is
       immune to mercy

a fatherless son laughing
       too obscenely not to be broken
watches from the asphalt which boils hot
       enough to scald shoeless skin

meanwhile the glasses dream of flight
       they have seen geese do it—
a hundred of them at once—scourging
       the air with whip-sharp cracks

they will themselves against this needling light
       while above all is chaos: a stranger
lugs the glasses' missing boy onto the pool's deck
       sea serpents swarm the water where

the bully threw him casting panicked
       waves in all directions
he is a son blinded and fearful
       and it will take a father to draw

his sight from the pool this is what
       the bully hates most a daddy
who gives vision who straightens
       ringlets of the sob-wracked head

but the bully has made the water
      a lexicon of dangers
how will the parents ever explain that
      bitterness spreads its roots

why a boy like a sun-stippled goose
      battled what would bind him
and lost—a grave gravity which to drowned eyes
      changed the father to worms to hair

III.

ELEGY AFTER *THE SEA OF ICE*, 1823

In a better world things might have been different
       a fairer wind a trimmer sail but no such luck

the wind did its work and the captain too
       you're cut to the heart and stilted:

all that's left of you gored worse still: help is unlikely
       rescue is foreign to this place

every hour tender Christ who we love is bloodied
       by stigmata stygian worms inch his wrist

(what color one mother whispers)
       deeper into the Kunsthalle before the Moderns

Marc's elephant begs time's stubborn arrow to move
       while one tired child cries into his father's flannel

not for you he is a clock like thirst or lymphoma
       the father sings to him in a low voice

the boy will spend his life trying not to forget
       but name a thing time defers

one way or another so confined you become
       a figure for the lost but always accessible

like Mao's body my father would add
       if he weren't feathered with tubes to grant him breath

I am learning to live with the patina of panic
       that graces you at all hours

you as hashtag on the tour maps
       daily a hundred hands and none to mend

Father's Brain Scan Seen as Bomber Cutaway Model and Bomber History

Settle turret stanchions in position

you start on the patient table
the part everyone knows (easy)

pitch the dorsal aerial mast upright

what's tougher is pretending
this isn't measuring you for
a casket the ones behind the
glass aren't coroners—will they
need an autopsy when you are
this sick—

careful because even a crack thin
as a vein exposes musculature to
crushing pressure

honestly these neuroses are
mostly what will occupy you
while the coils sing a round (or
is it the magnets) a chorus so
different from your children
who declare you're going to be
fine to no one at all

the distance between safe flight
and implosion is a matter of screws

like you aren't on the verge
of breaking into a hundred
vectors of light consider human
resilience—yours or the guy
who designed the bore—who
did he love enough to approach

the sturdy hold of rivets she's
a flying fortress

death daily in such a familiar
way remember those black
and white reels—eighth
grade history—where
bombardiers loosed tons of
explosives onto villages so
casual no sound just the dust
resettled pleasantly in a halo

in this image we've peeled skin
to reveal a honeycomb of light
and iridescent beams

and damage such carnage:
what lay beyond didn't
interest the filmmakers really
so they jump cut to some
other village the barracks
where the good guys were
spooning grits

so few of these birds left
that reconstruction is guesswork

these sort of memories are
common in the tube the
doctor will tell you but hear
me

experts believe this is
as close as we'll get to what's
under the hood

how little of you can survive
let all but what fledges burn
away

WATCHING HOARDERS WITH MY FATHER

Anne has fifty crates of antique cat's eyes
Ray says he invented the power source
for the Voyager 2 that's why
he needs fifty rusted junkers it's obvious
Doris can do without the swimwear
flamed lime with mildew thirty
Maltese puppies coiled in a planter
Jim lost his mother Chastity
drank a handle of Beam a day
mouthwash when cash ran out
you're a Nikon panning
her hallway fireworks burst
like blood from a buckshot wound
the night Cindy's son drove
off the overpass she keeps
his photo on the bureau
above forty pounds of diatomaceous
earth to ward away ants away
silver fish away roaches like careless
travelers on a highway
Don knows his wife
is leaving either way
Rhonda is just another
object with this filter Randy
is fifty pinball machines Smokey
is two teeth and a stained nightshirt
Dan can't imagine transcending
he is a cluttered cage
peppered with droppings
a ragged cast iron consider this
pan over Ron's kitchen

listen to this audio
where Wendy finally breaks
we'll splice this in the credits
she thought she'd die
in this house at a certain angle
she's just her hoops
we're this smoky gaze watching
the room fill up Anne draws the shades
to stop anyone from looking

Self-Portrait
with Dog Crapping in Snow

He squats in the rain-drowned weeds staring
back along the leash that bonds us

I try to focus on the broken chain link vaulted
by a gray fox back to the stream's cut

back beyond limits of my sight
I watch the ripples in the dark

as his tail becomes a ghost's beard then just a tense
shadow what did he see in me what threat

did he misread in a language only instinct knows
now there is just a man and a dog traced across

acrylic snow both of us curious about this wilderness
which has kept to its boundary but for these pellets

what can I teach you when I have no instinct
just psalms and blessings bless the careless

art all animals leave all blood and dung
bless where decay does not live long

we share so little just this need carried out
in solemn ritual we turn

different senses on the doughy pines
marking off our territories

Drawing Whistler's Mother

He began in black
        mimicking the Thames
frozen and dark in the locks
        where the jewelweed
stilled as though wind itself
        could sleep inside a portrait
without time without teasing
        those green digits to life
the summer muggy
        and locusts on every
damned thing

imagine the guilt of seeing
        her honestly her whole body
helpless with wrath
        he wanted her to look
as she did: an unforgiving
        flashflood that threatens
to envelope levies
        wet the walls in black mold
like the skin of a hemophiliac
        where bruises command
whole flanks along the hands

her coughs were bats
        in the chimney
their slack skin pattered
        the studio like a weak pulse
so he learned to work diurnal
        don gloves thrust
a frock over her bowed head
        to conceal her landscape of moles

those final days harnessing
her like a trained oxen
        a choking smell
of ether fluming the house

smothering till what to do
        but hold his nose
what wounds work this heart
        these joints like raving mouths
he swore *flesh*
        alone testifies

Watching a Cialis Ad with My Father

The man adoring his wife adores her
more as she torques her hips to return the serve

she is regal as heat lightning seething from the court
I know how he feels wanting to work

each swollen muscle with his finger blunt
as a sculptor's pitcher but these aren't the hands

of Michelangelo they are the hands of a CPA
or a hospice patient or as the ad suggests a man

walking a terrier on a beach (jump cut
to a shot of their fingers twined against

the sun shimmering below the schism
of salt-veined sky and black stones)

their ordinariness is the point
so their problems are shadows of our own

but what is it that drives any of us
the words scrolling by sterile as sand can't say

whether it's ego or devotion
it can't answer whether what follows minutes

later under sanctity of doctor-recommended pills
is an act out of passion or rote practice

what proof can anyone offer
but these sweated sheets pentimento

of the most fervid sculptors
blind to all but what they make

Something Beautiful

If tools could make another noise
        they should belt out show tunes
             my father tells me

less scraping more *Chicago*
        the drill echoing
             in the alley of your larynx

could be *Cats* or the syncopated
        snaps of Jets and Sharks

think how a scaler
        might deliver "À la volonté du people"—
        the pliers as French tenors
             Inspector Javert's soliloquy

playing in your mouth today
        the ad could read
             it's an idea so brilliant
             someone must have already tried

because what are we working for
        if not more joy to forget
             the busted skin and x-rays
             the mechanical whine of this world

what mouth feels unnatural filled
        with song even if it's another voice
             an unfamiliar machine

gifted the pipes of Astaire or Andrews
      who could it reason surely
           would agree these hills are alive

the enflamed gums as clouds
      the tongue dancing across
      like taps on marble clacking
          in rhythm on the chorus
          hitting the high notes

STILL-LIFE AFTER NEW YEAR'S WITH TOY BOAT

The toy yacht harbored by ice
     is the moon's ghost
          in the first dark of this new year

I imagine getting up
     with icepick and gloves

to dredge its hull mend
     what canvas sails frost

hasn't rendered too callous
     to pin and thread

it's work to start anew now
     beside the boat you downward

dog you ignore the music
     of your tibia

you are going to Denver
     going to L.A. going

without us to salute
     the sun as it makes bangles
          teasing up the purple sand

the loneliest people have
     the sea to touch

and this hour when brown grasses
　　　hold vigil I watch wind bow
　　　　　　row after row their tips

bobbing like hands
　　　broken at the wrists
　　　　　　a gale fills the sails flexing

then releasing and for a moment
　　　I swear I know how new life

breathes into being
　　　how vigor nearly tugs
　　　　　　rigs from holds

in this: a trace of peace

for what choice for this breath
　　　which slugs the bended grass

what choice for that flesh
　　　beaten and beating but
　　　　　　to weather what comes next

Portrait of My Grandfather in Haiti

The year my hoarder aunt stored
four cartons of porcelain Gabriels

in his basement is the year my grandfather
died she squirreled them in the breezeway

where he kept busted bearings old nails
no junkyard would work

while we panned sawdust coarse as ice
my aunt packed hundreds of rain-damaged

angels a palate of dismembered baby dolls
and one image of the living God

all but his suits which she orphaned
in grandma's walk-in fine double-breasted

they still held his musk he'd kept the chalky blue
the army issued him for his brother's burial its cuffs

rouged by clay a landscape soap and water
could not erode aphid-ridden dress shirts

no charity would take but *they deserve a second life*
pleaded my grandmother she ordered what insects

hadn't husked off to Haiti with a band of missionaries
I can't imagine who would wear another's tatters

but what deprivation have I lived before now
here in our country it is so easy to think oneself

the victim on the disc of music they mailed her
I still hear the ocean behind the tambore

I hear a man's voice thrill to a silver trumpet's wail
then thin to a macaw's squall what reaches her

the voices of men dressed in someone
else's grief rise rise over the black mirror

of water should I envy it—how it holds one
form and fearless lets go

A Guide to Falling Down Stairs

You'll need dollar store flip-flops
   the shabbier the better you'll need

a black Glad bag a busted porchlight
   you'll want a fine char on the cutlets

so set the burner to high before you step
   onto the porch listen to it simper

the cicadas fulmination like meat
   spitting in cast iron they are mallets

planishing an unseen anvil you'll want
   to savor this because what follows

is hell descending elbow to cement
   toenails wrenched on the rails

down to the frozen bottom and
   nothing to do there but wail

to the 1 AM stars who might
   have been regal but for this gash

you are Sisyphus shoving
   the cumbersome boulder of your body

against the iron rail
   what a relief somehow

to watch bruises fan out like ink on rice paper
   finally a pain you can finger

think of your father miles away
    a maze of cables and drips

his lungs swell with fluid no doctor
    can show you can't spoon out

and if you really listen they are not mallets
    but a heart monitor that you measure

against your own and must somehow live
    on rise up and ascend

NOTES

"Viewing *The Tribute Money*, My Father Thinks of His Wife" refers to *The Tribute Money* by Masaccio, 1425.

"On Size and Scope in *The Arnolfini Portrait*" refers to *The Arnolfini Portrait* by Jan van Eyck, 1434.

"Envisioning My Grandfather in the Shadow of Hopper's Lighthouse" refers to *Lighthouse Hill* by Edward Hopper, 1927.

"Rain, Steam, and Speed" refers to *Rain, Steam and Speed—The Great Western Railway* by William Turner, 1844.

"Deaths of the Virgin" refers to *Death of the Virgin* by Michelangelo Merisi Caravaggio, 1605.

"The Girl Picking Verbena in the Valley Below the Tower of Babel" refers to *The Tower of Babel* by Pieter Bruegel the Elder, 1563.

"Self-Portrait as Butcher" refers to *Judith Beheading Holofernes* by Artemisia Gentileschi, 1614.

"Elegy after The Sea of Ice, 1823" refers to *The Sea of Ice* by Caspar David Friedrich, 1823.

"Drawing Whistler's Mother" refers to *Arrangement in Grey and Black No.1* by James McNeill Whistler, 1871.

Acknowledgements

(Poems sometimes appeared under different titles)

The Account – "Elegy After *The Sea of Ice*, 1823"

AGNI – "My Father Considering His Brain Scan as Lunar Disaster" and "I Consider My Father's Brain Scan as Jazz Measure"

Briar Cliff Review – "Portrait of Lost Glasses"

Copper Nickel – "On Size and Scope in *The Arnolfini Portrait*"

Crazyhorse – "Tarrare After the Hospital" and "Portrait of My Grandfather in Haiti"

Forklift, Ohio – "On the Drive Home from My Father's Surgery"

The Gettysburg Review – "My Father Considering His Brain Scan"

Harpur Palate – "Something Beautiful"

Indiana Review – "Chemo"

JuxtaProse – "The Girl Picking Verbena in the Valley Below the Tower of Babel" and "Self-Portrait as Butcher"

The Kenyon Review – "Self-Portrait at Eighteen Revisted at Thirty"

The Laurel Review – "Watching *Hoarders* with My Father" and "Watching a Cialis Ad with My Father *the minnesota review* – "Gas Leak Shutters Furries Convention"

Ninth Letter – "Ephemera" and "Envisioning My Grandfather in the Shadow of Hopper's Lighthouse"

Passages North – "My Father Considering His Brain Scan as the Moon Titan"

Pleiades – "A Lesson in Drawing" and "A Guide to Falling Down Stairs"

Shenandoah – "Drawing Whistler's Mother"

Southwest Review – "Portrait of a Sideswiped Doe"

Tupelo Quarterly – "Rain, Steam, and Speed" and "Father's Brain Scan Seen as Bomber Cutaway Model and Bomber History"

Waxwing – "Self-Portrait with Dog Crapping in Snow"

About the Author

Kyle McCord is the author of five books of poetry, including National Poetry Series Finalist *Magpies in the Valley of Oleanders* (Trio House Press, 2016). He has work featured in *AGNI, Blackbird, Boston Review, The Gettysburg Review, The Harvard Review, The Kenyon Review, Ploughshares, TriQuarterly,* and elsewhere. He has received grants or awards from The Academy of American Poets, The Vermont Studio Center, and the Baltic Writing Residency. He serves as Co-Executive Editor of Gold Wake Press. He teaches at Drake University in Des Moines, where he lives with his wife, visual artist Lydia McCord, and son, August.

About the Book

Cleave was designed at Trio House Press through the collaboration of:

Matt Mauch, Lead Editor
Tayve Neese, Supporting Editor
Lea C. Deschenes, Interior Design
Nick Courtright, Cover Design

The text is set in Adobe Caslon Pro.

The publication of this book is made possible, whole or in part,
by the generous support of the following individuals and/or agencies:

Anonymous

About the Press

Trio House Press is a collective press. Individuals within our organization come together and are motivated by the primary shared goal of publishing distinct American voices in poetry. All THP published poets must agree to serve as Collective Members of the Trio House Press for twenty-four months after publication in order to assist with the press and bring more Trio books into print. Award winners and published poets must serve on one of four committees: Production and Design, Distribution and Sales, Educational Development, or Fundraising and Marketing. Our Collective Members reside in cities from New York to San Francisco.

Trio House Press adheres to and supports all ethical standards and guidelines outlined by the CLMP.

Trio House Press, Inc., is dedicated to the promotion of poetry as literary art, which enhances the human experience and its culture. We contribute in an innovative and distinct way to American Poetry by publishing emerging and established poets, providing educational materials, and fostering the artistic process of writing poetry. For further information, or to consider making a donation to Trio House Press, please visit us online at: www.triohousepress.org.

Other Trio House Press Books you might enjoy:

Two Towns Over by Darren C. Demaree
        2017 Trio Award Winner selected by Campbell McGrath

Bird~Brain by Matt Mauch, 2017

Dark Tussock Moth by Mary Cisper
        2016 Trio Award Winner selected by Bhisham Bherwani

Break the Habit by Tara Betts, 2016

Bone Music by Stephen Cramer
        2015 Louise Bogan Award selected by Kimiko Hahn

*Rigging a Chevy into a Time Machine and Other Ways
        to Escape a Plague* by Carolyn Hembree
        2015 Trio Award Winner selected by Neil Shepard

Magpies in the Valley of Oleanders by Kyle McCord, 2015

Your Immaculate Heart by Annmarie O'Connell, 2015

The Alchemy of My Mortal Form by Sandy Longhorn
        2014 Louise Bogan Winner selected by Carol Frost

What the Night Numbered by Bradford Tice
     2014 Trio Award Winner selected by Peter Campion

Flight of August by Lawrence Eby
     2013 Louise Bogan Winner selected by Joan Houlihan

The Consolations by John W. Evans
     2013 Trio Award Winner selected by Mihaela Moscaliuc

Fellow Odd Fellow by Steven Riel, 2013

Clay by David Groff
     2012 Louise Bogan Winner selected by Michael Waters

Gold Passage by Iris Jamahl Dunkle
     2012 Trio Award Winner selected by Ross Gay

If You're Lucky Is a Theory of Mine by Matt Mauch, 2012

CPSIA information can be obtained
at www.ICGtesting.com
Printed in the USA
FSHW010231140119
54850FS